INTRODUCTION TO ONLINE SAFETY

A practical guide to Cybersecurity

JOHN G. JACOB

Disclaimer

All the contents in this book are intended for learning purposes. Please refrain from using the instructions in this book to hack somebody for malicious intent or gains. Hacking could be a criminal offense when it is not done within the ambit of the law and the penalties for it could be devastating.

CONTENTS

ABOUT THE AUTHOR

John G. Jacob is a researcher and a cyber-security analyst with vast experience in information management, incident response, vulnerability assessment, compliance assistance and penetration testing. He holds a master's degree from Fort Hays State University, Kansas, USA where he also taught courses in Database Design and Programming. He is a member of the Information System Security Association (ISSA), KS chapter and a member of the Neustar International Security Council, UK. John is passionate about training individuals and organizations on safety measures in the ever-changing and unpredictable digital world. He resides in the US with his amiable wife, Claudine Remilekun Jacob. Please contact John on introtoonlinesafety@gmail.com

ACKNOWLEDGEMENT

I would like to give thanks to God for giving me the ideas and the opportunity to come up with this project. To God alone be all the glory. It is one thing to have a project, but it is another thing to have a good team to work with to get the project done. I would like to thank the team that helped me get this book edited and published, Nick Caya and his team, Mike Vik, Ton Schuller. I appreciate you all for your unflinching support in getting this book distributed across the globe. A big thanks to Dr. Rajin Koonjbearry and Dr. Tony Khan for their pieces of advice amidst their busy schedule. Many thanks to my mentor Dr. Adebola Olubanjo and his amiable wife for their support at all time. Thanks to mummy Kenny for her motherly roles, spiritual support, and mentorship, thanks to Mummy and Daddy Soyode for their support in all ramifications. God bless you all.

A huge thank you to my childhood friend Dr. James Yeku for all the incredible and amazing contributions he made towards the success of this book. I must thank Seun Abimbola and his good friend Oyinye for trying to understand the concept of the book and the piece of advice they gave and for editing the first part of the book. Thanks to Wale Olajumoke and his team for helping with the design of the book cover.

Many thanks to my friends who kept asking me a lot of questions about online safety. I must confess, they gave me the opportunity to birth the ideas of this book.

Finally, my family in the US and Nigeria, thank you for supporting me and for having so much confidence in me, thanks to Modeste Nkikabahizi and his wife Annonciata Narikujije for their parental advice, my mom and dad, you are highly appreciated. Thanks to my brothers and sisters.

This appreciation would not be complete without acknowledging the immense contribution of my lovely wife, Claudine R.D Jacob, thank you sweetheart for all your words of encouragement. Thanks so much for giving me the peace of mind to write this book and of course, for always encouraging me to further review the manuscript of this book, you are highly appreciated my love.

INTRODUCTION

Technology has undoubtedly changed the way we carry out different activities. We now live in a data-driven world with a countless number of computing gadgets. Our online presence and activities are monitored and stored by companies who will use such information in the future for advertisement purposes.

The expensive nature of information became a more popular knowledge after the last US election where Mark Zuckerberg, the CEO of Facebook, was accused of selling data to Cambridge Analytica on behalf of political clients without the consent of Facebook users. Zuckerberg was eventually fined by the Federal Trade Commission to the tune of $5 Billion for mishandling users' information.

What the Facebook story makes visible is that each time you are online, you are exposed to different dangers that can compromise your information and identity if not self-managed carefully. This situation plays into the realities of our time where information and data are more expensive than crude oil. Therefore, as you go about your different activities online, it is imperative to know that you have the right to privacy and security. I wrote this book so that you can have more knowledge on the security of data and information in this ever-changing computing world where nothing is predictable.

When the internet was initially invented, the world was conceived as a global village. Nowadays, with the way quantum of information travels across the globe, that idea has assumed a far richer meaning considering the rate at which our lives now largely depend on technology and the internet.

Email (Electronic mail), IM (Instant Message) and Social Media have replaced letter writing and E-News has replaced Newspapers and Magazine. Uber has replaced the local cab drivers and you can even have someone deliver food to your doorstep just by having the right app. The internet has morphed into a powerful tool which has simplified the way we carry out different task, while anyone reluctant to catch up will be left behind.

Recently, I mentioned to a colleague at work that the GPS (Global Positioning System) remains as one of the most important Apps that has been developed in recent times because of the way it makes movements and navigations easier. It is hard to contemplate traveling from Alabama to Illinois without the GPS.

The relevance of technology as an integral part of our daily existence cannot be overstated. It is a way of life. There will always be improvement in every area of the economy using technology. What do you think would happen if the internet was down all over the world for one day? There would be incalculable damage to businesses and to individuals. In fact, the world would be thrown into chaos.

Cloud-based services are indications that there will always be improvement in technology. We use smart devices in our homes and offices. It is important for us to protect our identities now that we have IoT and other improvement in technology to avoid being victims of cyber-crimes.

There are changes going on in every area of the economy because of Information Technology being used to improve the ways things are done. These days, everything is becoming automated using simple applications. There are automated interviews, e-payment, e-conversations, e-food, e-dating, e-marriage, etc. But this comes with a price. The application of technology to improve the way things are done will cause loss of jobs to machine learning, artificial intelligence, and virtual realities. To stay apprised of the ideas that undergird operations of new technology, users must be abreast of the latest news in the world of technology and keep researching what is in vogue.

How do you explain the fact that robots are taking over the hospitality industry? This is already happening in China and in some parts of the developed world, there are now robotic vacuum cleaners which can be powered using an app. How do you explain the concept of the ongoing discussion that there will soon be self-driving cars? Tesla is already in the market disrupting the automobile industries. With the advent of the IoT, you can connect all devices at home to your phone, there are apps such Onstar Remote Link, Toyota Entune etc. which you can use to control your car. Just imagine for a second that your device becomes compromised by a cybercriminal. This means that you would lose access to all the things you owe; your house, cars, and valuable documents just to mention a few.

Why do you need a teller when you can deposit and cash money via the ATM? There are many apps such as Cash App, Google Pay, PayPal, Zelle that are taking over banking jobs. I do not need to go to the bank to deposit a cheque, I can use my mobile app to do it and monitor the person working on the cheque at the bank. With the use of boss revolution app, I can transfer money to any African country account number, and it will reflect within few minutes.

Why do you need a Personal Assistant when you have a scheduler, a voice application, and Alexa can do a lot of tasks for you? Why do you need a travel agency when you can book your flight ticket yourself? What will be the work of a Human Resources Manager when a simple application has been developed to take care of their basic tasks? Spark-hire can interview anybody from any part of the world.

Think about how the latest business models operate and think about how they carry out their activities, Uber, Alibaba, Netflix, Airbnb, Tinder, Amazon, Facebook and many more. All these companies cannot operate without the internet.

These are a few disruptions that are happening in businesses around the world. The implication of using all the apps mentioned above and total transition of our life to the cloud and the IoT platform is that, as we depend more on the internet and technology, online criminals will always look for ways to hijack personal information and steal people's identities. According to the World Economic Forum, it is estimated that from 2019 to 2023, approximately $5.2 trillion in global value will be at risk from cyber-attacks.

This book exposes some of the day-to-day scams that happen online. It gives some essential security tips that can inform your safety online.

The future of technology cannot be predicted. It keeps evolving. Every area of our lives now revolves around information technology. The society and the economy are now wired in such a way that it will be difficult to survive without the internet. In view of this, companies and individuals need to make efforts to be protected from being exposed to online danger.

It is important to take precautionary measures to safeguard online identities while protecting passwords, apps, computers, money, files, emails, mobile devices, Wi-Fi, routers, and modems, etc. If you do not have the adequate knowledge on the technicalities involved in online safety, you can learn one or two things that could protect you from being vulnerable to online danger. This is part of the major focus of this book. Precaution is the focus of cybersecurity.

How cyber-criminals take advantage of events and people's vulnerability

The world is now being plagued by a deadly virus which has claimed many lives. The wide spread of this communicable disease and the way it spreads brought a drastic change to business operations which necessitated transition of businesses to an online platform to encourage business Continuity and a Backup Plan.

While Business Continuity and a Backup Plan are not something new, smaller businesses and big organizations had to technically join this trend to comply with the rules and regulations of the government to obey the idea of social distancing and isolation.

The government of each country disbanded social gathering, religious gathering, schools, companies and even Government parastatals were forced to work online. All the various activities from each of these bodies were moved online to ensure business continuity. When it became obvious that many organizations have transitioned online, cybercriminals started coming up with a different phishing campaign to scam people of their hard-earned money through the following methods:

1. The Coronavirus Map
2. Zoom-bombing
3. Spam calls

The Coronavirus Map

Immediately there was an outbreak of COVID-19, cyber-criminals quickly came up with the Coronavirus Map to give live updates on the number of people that have the virus all over the world. Although, the map was calculating the genuine number of cases, but the major idea of this fake app was to steal people's credentials.

The Coronavirus Map is a malware spreading app infecting the computer and phones of unsuspected users to steal passwords and other sensitive information. It is a Trojan horse that install malware into the machine or computer to gain unauthorized access to sensitive information. This Trojan horse installs malware into the machine to steal cookies, passwords, browsing history and cache of the computer which can be used to break into sensitive information of the user. The fake Coronavirus map was developed to mimic that of the John Hopkin's centre, so it was difficult for people to tell it apart from the original map.

The Image of the Coronavirus Map

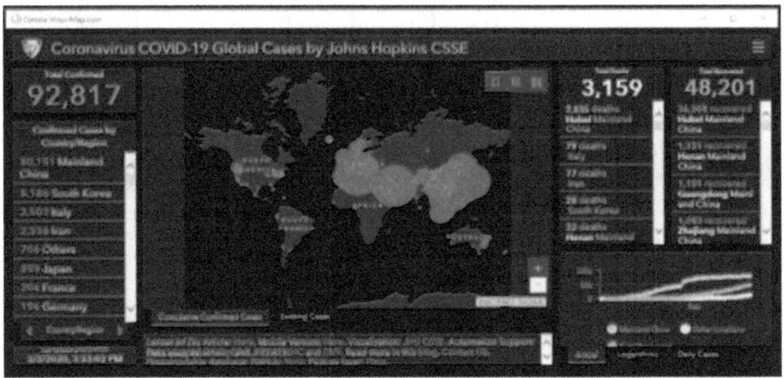

Source: Johns Hopkins CSSE

Application bombing:

This is one of the new tricks that scammers used to take advantage of unsuspected victims when they transitioned online because of COVID-19. They are still using this method of attack. Application bombing occurs when an uninvited person joins a Zoom, Skype, Goto-meeting, or a Team meeting in the hope of sharing offensive materials such as sex tape/nude picture or probably to hijack the session from the host to have access to sensitive information. Application-bombing is common with Zoom, it is not actually a security flaw, but this has to do with a poor management of links received by invited people to a meeting on applications.

Once an application bomber has access to a meeting, he can destroy the meeting session by sharing things that are an eyesore. If it is a Zoom platform that is being bombed, this art becomes Zoom-bombing, if it is Teams, it becomes Teams-becoming, etc.

Application bombing is a serious offence in the United states and people could go to jail for it. The best way to deal with application bombing is with the use of the security features available in the application as stated below and informing the prospective user of the platform before the meeting, never to allow anyone to have access to their meeting link and this could be done by safe guarding all computing devices.

The image below shows where you can enable security settings on Zoom.

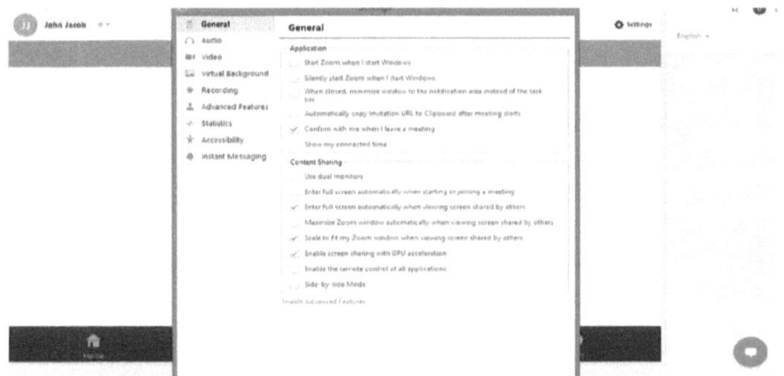

Source: Zoom

The following security settings should specifically be enabled by the host from the advanced features to have more control of a Zoom meeting.

1. Mute participants upon entry
2. Show meeting control bar
3. Identify guest participant in the meeting/ Webinar
4. Waiting room – Until the host takes in participant, they should be in the waiting room, this is a new feature that is enabled by default as of May 2020
5. Requirement for password when scheduling a new meeting

The image below shows where you can enable security settings on Teams.

Source: Microsoft Teams

Spam calls: This includes Phishing(email) smishing (text message) and vishing (Phone calls). This is a form of scam that occurs when a scammer tries to get a prospective victim to share personal financial information. As a result of the pandemic, below are some of the messages people got from scammers:

1. If you want to receive a free testing kit delivered to your house, press 1
2. We can qualify you to get a free diabetic monitor and complimentary testing kit for Coronavirus
3. In response to the recent shortage of surgical masks, the Red Cross will be giving one free box per household click http://

RedCross-facemask.ca to get, credit cards are being asked for donation for shipping

The three examples above were some of the tricks the bad guys used during the first stage of the pandemic to scam unsuspected users. These are typical examples of how scammers take advantage of a situation or occurrence to rip people off their hard-earned money. There will always be occurrence of events, and cyber-criminals know this but the best way to stay safe online would be to follow some of the key points that will be explained in this.

It does not really matter if you are educated or not, anybody can be a victim of an online scam. The best way to protect yourself from becoming a victim is to stay informed on the latest online safety precautions and keep all your devices updated.

The most challenging thing about technology is that things change all the time. It will be good to understand that not all online attacks require coding. You can be outsmarted by a simple trick irrespective of your level of education. An attack that requires coding can still be done by a non-expert because there are script kiddies who are not expert in coding but who can copy codes and manipulate the internet with software to gain access to your information.

Stay connected as you go through some of the key points in this book.

WHY YOU NEED THIS BOOK

1. 93% of cybersecurity breaches and identity theft are due to human error. When you follow some of the security and privacy precautions in this book you would reduce the risk of falling victim to online scams, identity theft and information hijacking online.

2. According to the Cisco newly renamed annual report, networked devices around the globe are estimated to be 29.3 billion by 2023. The Symantec Internet Security Reported that there are 25 connected devices per 100 inhabitants in the US. The implication is that most of your activities will rely more on the internet, so you need knowledge on how to safeguard yourself and your equipment.

3. The Chairman of IBM, President and CEO, Gini Rometty, said that Cybercrime is the greatest threat to every company in the world, but it is not just to a company but by extension to humans because of

the expensive nature of information. You need to be safe before your devices are safe. The security of your devices relies on your safety.

CHAPTER ONE

HOW THE INTERNET WORKS

A few years back, while teaching an introductory lesson in my computer science class, I decided to engage my students in a learning activity. So, I asked them, "Who owns the internet?"

The question elicited a lot of funny responses. A student had said, to the disagreement of other students, that it was God. Interestingly, a larger percentage of the class voted that the government owns the internet.

Now, if you were to indulge me, who would you say also owns the internet? Does God truly own the internet or the government?

By way of simple definition, the internet is the global connection of computers with different and unique numbers called the TCP/IP Addresses which stands for Transmission Control Protocol over Internet Protocol Addresses. It is usually abbreviated as the IP Address (xxx.xxxx.xxx).

The Internet Protocol, on the other hand, is a set of rules that govern the wireless communication of devices. An example of Internet Protocols includes Simple Mail Transfer Protocol (SMTP), File Transfer Protocol (FTP), Hypertext Transfer Protocol (HTTP) and TELNET, among others.

The computer is always connected through the ISP (The Internet Service Providers). Connecting to the ISP requires two fundamental things to make it work: there is hardware for connectivity such as modem, working cable line, as well as software such as protocols to govern connection and data flow.

Each ISP has a unique set of addresses to give out to any device that is connected to the internet. The IP address can be a static or a dynamic IP address. The common language of the Internet is the TCP/IP. The TCP/IP is a logical model that provides standards for communication in networking.

The internet makes use of cables and wireless routers to transmit signals. To see the IP Address of a website, you can perform a ping operation on your computer by typing out the URL (Uniform Resource Locator) into the Command Prompt or the Command Line Interface (CLI) whether from a Windows or LINUX Operating system. E.g. ping www.brosjay.com. You can perform a lot of tasks on the Command Prompt.

What the ping command does is to find out if your device is on a network, that is, the internet network.

To enter the Command Line Interface (CLI) mode for a Windows Operating System: Win+X and then press C: This brings up the Command Prompt in normal mode. For a Linux Operating system, open a Linux Terminal Using Ctrl+ Alt +T.

172.217.12.68 is the IP address for google.com. Open a browser and type in that IP address where you should have the URL, it will take you to the landing page of Google. You would also notice that it changes immediately to www.google.com.

```
Microsoft Windows [Version 6.3.9600]
(c) 2013 Microsoft Corporation. All rights reserved.

C:\Users\circl_000>pinggoogle.com
'pinggoogle.com' is not recognized as an internal or external command,
operable program or batch file.

C:\Users\circl_000>ping www.google.com

Pinging www.google.com [172.217.12.68] with 32 bytes of data:
Reply from 172.217.12.68: bytes=32 time=62ms TTL=53
Reply from 172.217.12.68: bytes=32 time=62ms TTL=53
Reply from 172.217.12.68: bytes=32 time=65ms TTL=53
Reply from 172.217.12.68: bytes=32 time=52ms TTL=53

Ping statistics for 172.217.12.68:
    Packets: Sent = 4, Received = 4, Lost = 0 (0% loss),
Approximate round trip times in milli-seconds:
    Minimum = 52ms, Maximum = 65ms, Average = 60ms
```

Command line Interface

Source: Windows OS

Ping   www.Google.com
        Command Uniform Resource Locator

Contrary to popular opinion that someone owns the internet, nobody owns the internet. The internet is a global network of computers with different IP Addresses which are networked to communicate with one another using different protocols and IP Addresses. We cannot conclude that the ISP (The Internet Service Providers) own the internet because they supply cables and networking devices that the internet runs on.

If someone truly owns the internet, then it can be controlled but unfortunately the internet cannot be controlled, so nobody owns it. The internet is just a concept which is not actually a tangible entity, it is the network of networks.

Note: In this book, the focus is on Windows Operating system. This is because Windows is the most preferred operating system among users.

CHAPTER TWO

THE INTERNET PROTOCOL ADDRESS

An IP Address is a specific label or tag used to identify a device on a computer network. Any device connected to a network has an IP Address. The IP Address can generally be viewed as a unique number assigned to devices on a computer network. It shows the location of the device connected to the network; one can get the location of any website from the IP address.

Electronic devices on a network interact using the IP address. An IP Address is different from the MAC address of a device. The MAC address of a device shows which device is connected to the network, while the IP address shows the location of the device on the network. To make it clearer, imagine a post office mail that does not have a house address, it is obvious that the mail cannot be delivered anywhere, so an IP address shows which location a device that is present in a network communicating from.

As referenced in the introduction, all websites have IP addresses and that is why an attacker can ping a URL from the Command Line Interface to get the IP to perform a LOIC (Low Orbit Ion Cannon) attack or DDoS (Distributed Denial of Service) attack to disrupt a computer or multiple computers depending on the attacker's motivation.

Importance of the IP Address

It is important to protect your IP address. If it is hacked, you may become vulnerable to a lot of threat. It can be used to track your location and your ISP (Internet Service Provider) information through. One of the sites where tracking can happen is WHOIS.NET.

It is advisable to always set up your internet configuration with a strong encryption such as WPA2. Most ISPs use the dynamic IP Addresses because it is cheaper. It is more expensive to set up the static IP addressing system. While the dynamic

IP address such as the Dynamic Host Configuration Protocol (DHCP) is good because it changes from time to time, it is advisable for dynamic IP to be protected, it might stay for a month before it changes.

An IP Address can be stolen to download illegal content like pirated movies or be used, quite possibly too, to visit the deep or the dark web to buy illegal product. You only have access to 1% of the internet. The remaining 99% part of the internet is on the deep web and this is where criminals use a stolen IP Address to operate and carry out illicit acts. Note that the deep web is different from the dark web; the dark web is a subset of the deep web.

The distributed denial of service attack (DDoS) often uses a stolen IP address to shut down your access to the internet, and you could be arrested if someone uses your IP address to do something illegal. A hacker can be in the US and change their IP to that of the UK, they do this manually or by using a VPN that offers a dynamic IP such as Proton-VPN.

How to protect your IP address

1. Change the privacy setting on your Wi-fi (Ask your ISP).

2. Change the privacy setting on your browser.
3. Use a Virtual Private network e.g. IP Vanish, Proton-VPN (This has all the IP in the world), NORD VPN.
4. Change to dynamic IP address.
5. Update firewall of your router and computer.
6. Never use a static IP address except you have full control.
7. You can also use a proxy server to hide or protect an IP although it is mostly used by companies to block the site that they do not want employees to visit.

Note: This link: https://lite.ip2location.com/ip-address-ranges-by-country contains all the IPs of different countries, it has 249 countries' IP Addresses. IP2Location is where many hackers pick the IP if they want to disguise the location. Always ensure you use dynamic IP from your ISP and not the static IP that could probably be picked by a hacker. Your IP changes with a dynamic IP but it must still be protected, as hackers are always finding different ways to boycott security protocol on different devices.

CHAPTER THREE

THE ANATOMY OF A CYBERCRIME/ CYBER-ATTACK

A cyber-crime does not just happen; it requires extensive research. Cyber-criminals carry out a lot of findings before entering the world of their victim. Reconnaissance is the first stage of any attack, whether cybercrime or cyber-attack.

Since a cyber-criminal tries a lot of tricks to find information about whoever he wants to scam, he focuses on observation and the sorting of information to locate someone. This is what Reconnaissance means. The success of a cyber-criminal's observations and fact finding will determine if the attack will be easy or not. Therefore, you need to be very careful about what you share online.

Stages of Cyber-crime anatomy

1. **Reconnaissance:** Investigations, survey, or exploration of the victim.
2. **Enumeration:** Determining the best method of attack e.g. Spear phishing, baiting, Spoofing, Vishing, Pharming, Whaling etc.
3. **Penetration:** This is where the cyber-criminal uses the actual tool. There are countless numbers of tools that bad guys use to perform penetration including credit card scam, job scam, online dating, Malware attack, etc.
4. **Clean up:** Flushing all data, logs and information used for the crime to avoid being caught during investigation by a forensic examiner.

The above is just a summary of how a cyber-criminal operates. Typically, each stage involves some expatiations and technicality depend on what kind of attack the person is trying to perform.

Case study

Tola, a real estate investor, has just received a huge sum of money in his bank account from selling one of his properties. He decided to post a screenshot of the credit alert on his Instagram page during a live video session as evidence and to encourage a group of people he was talking to about real estate and how lucrative it can be if using the methods contained in his online training manual.

Tola meant no harm, he was only using the screenshot as a marketing strategy to sell his business. Unknown to Tola, one of the people he was talking to was a cyber-criminal. Tola was smart enough not reveal the name of his bank in the screenshot. The criminal decided to search out more information on Tola.

The Cyber-criminal Reconnaissance Format: The criminal decided to search for Tola on all social media platforms to gain more information about him.

Social Media platforms are:

1.   Facebook
2.   Instagram
3.   Twitter
4.   Snapchat

5. LinkedIn

Unfortunately for Tola, he did not use any security and privacy setting on his Facebook and LinkedIn profile. This means that anyone can search and get information about him. Since he had no security feature in place, the criminal went through all of Tola's posts on Facebook and was able to get the following information:

1. The bank he uses: Tola had made virtual complaints and rants about his bank's excessive charges on many posts.
2. The school he graduated from: This was directly on his profile.
3. His wife's information: This was from his relationship status.
4. The company he works for: This was from the information about him.
5. His date of birth: This was from the information about him.

The criminal did not get his email on Facebook, he proceeded to look up his LinkedIn profile which also had no security setting in place. On his LinkedIn profile, the scammer was able to get his email address, phone number and the contacts of some of his friends.

The Cyber-criminal Enumeration Format:

The criminal decided to use the spear phishing and pharming attack and then sent the screenshot below to Tola.

Note that this is one example of how a cyber-crime can be executed. This does not automatically mean that the cyber-criminal could not have used other means to sweep everything in Tola's account. You will find other forms of cyber-crime explained in other chapters of the book.

The Cybercriminal Penetration Format:

Z-shadow was the tool used by the criminal for this crime. Another platform could have also been used.

Google

Someone has your password

Hi Tola,

Someone just used your password to try to sign in to your Google Account

tolaolokooba@gmail.com

Details:
Saturday, 19 March, 8:34:30 UTC
IP Address: 134.249.139.239
Location: Ukraine

Google stopped this sign-in attempt. You should change your password immediately.

CHANGE PASSWORD

Best,
The Gmail Team

You received this mandatory email service announcement to update you about important changes to your Google product or account.

Source: Google Chrome

The spear phishing email sent by the cybercriminal.

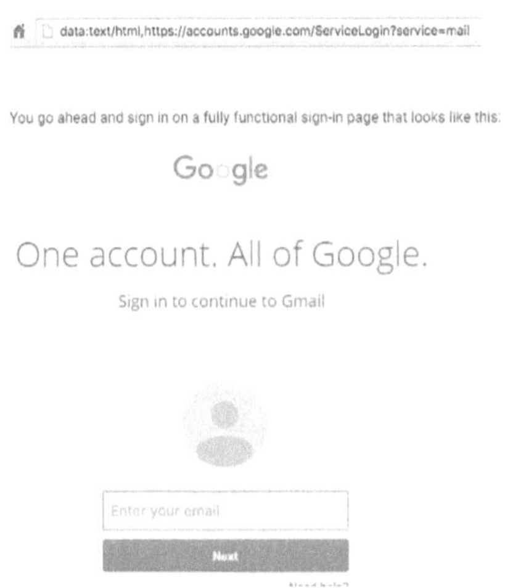

Source: Google Chrome

The phished landing page Tola was linked to from his Google account. If you check the URL of this page carefully, you will know that it is not the real Google URL.

The Cyber-criminal Clean up Format

Now, Tola feels he has changed his password but unknown to him, he has led the scammer directly into his e-mail where he was able to get his e-statement of his account and also access his Google Drive to steal the password to his bank account number and subsequently wire all his money to another account. The Scammer completed the entire process through a virtual computer (VirtualBox) which he deleted immediately after he finished the process.

Precautions

1. There is no way you can avoid sharing your information on LinkedIn, especially if you are looking for a job, but you can always be careful about what you share. Use security settings available on the social media website to control who can have access to you.

2. A lot of information can be gathered from your thoughts on social media, be guided on what you post. Keep in mind that the internet does not forget and what you post today can haunt you tomorrow.

3. Avoid using your real name to set up social media accounts if you are creating the page for fun. Some employers now use your social media activity as a yardstick to make vital recruitment decisions. Current employers also use this to determine the

personality of their employees as part of performance evaluation for promotion.

4. Use different passwords for your social media pages.

5. Be selective with friend request. If you do not know the person, do not accept the request.

6. Always password protect your device when it is not in use e.g. Phone, Computer, Phablet, Tablet, etc.

7. Ensure that all apps on your device are kept updated. You can use www.patchmypc/ download to keep your computer updated.

8. Do not click on any link you are not familiar with. If you need to change your password for any reason, change it directly from the website of the company or the service provider e.g. Google, banks, IRS portal, Insurance company, etc.

9. Use privacy and security settings at all times.

10. Your reputation is your greatest asset, protect it at all times.

CHAPTER FOUR

WHY INCOGNITO DOES NOT GUARANTEE SAFE BROWSING

Have you noticed that when you search the Internet to purchase an item, you will subsequently start receiving adverts and offers of similar products popping up from your browser? It is particularly annoying when you get on your Facebook timeline and find adverts of the items you had inquired about on a Google search. This is because your ISPs sell information to companies to help them advertise their products.

They monitor your activities online to ensure targeted marketing. Most people assume that when you browse in incognito mode, your activities will not be traced by your ISPs and companies. This is not the case.

Incognito is a feature in the Chrome browser that is used to hide what is being stored locally on the computer. It does not keep all activities secret. It clears cookies, cache and browsing history only locally on your device but it does not stop advertisers and your ISPs from viewing what you have been doing online.

It is called private browsing when one uses a browser such as Mozilla Firefox, but it is not called Incognito Mode. You can still see the information of what you viewed in the PC DNS (Personal Computer-Domain Name Server) cache memory with the respective website IP addresses.

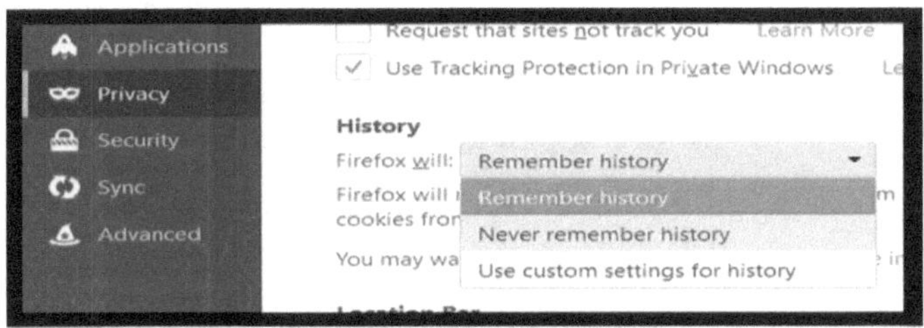

Source: Mozilla Firefox

Private Mode: Mode that does not save browsing history, cookies, site data locally.

Source: Mozilla Firefox.

If you are concerned about privacy and security, use browsers such as Brave, Tor, Pale Moon, Water Fox, DuckDuckGo with a good VPN, or always use the command prompt below to flush your URL and reset your IP Address from the command prompt if you don't have a VPN or proxy setting on your browser.

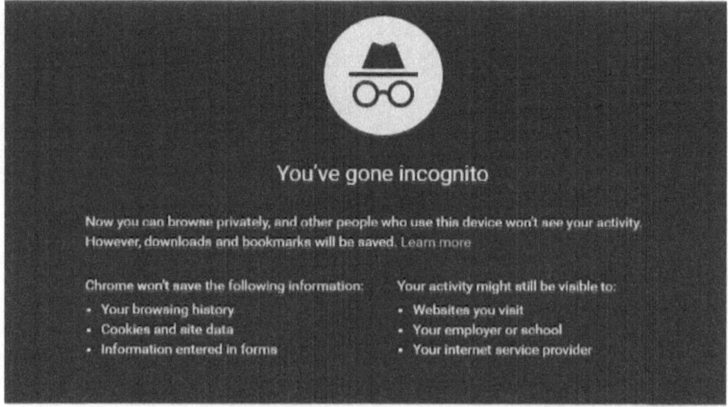

Incognito: Mode that does not save browsing history, cookies, site data locally.

Source: Google Chrome.

To go incognito, use the three dotted line at the upper right part of your Chrome browser and choose incognito from the list.

To go Private on your Mozilla Firefox browser, go to the three lines by the right-hand corner, then choose the privacy protection tab, check the protection level at the top then click to see other options.

1. To check all the URL, you visited: ipconfig/displaydns then press enter
2. To erase all URL to block advert: ipconfig/flushdns then press enter
3. To remove current IP assignment: ipconfig/release
4. To get new IP Assignment: ipconfig/renew

CHAPTER FIVE

THE DIFFERENCE BETWEEN CYBER-CRIME AND CYBER-ATTACK

Cyber-law is the law that is concerned with issues relating to technology, electronic components, communication devices, internet, hardware, software, and data framework. Cyber law is governed by different IT Acts in different countries because of the development of technology and the importance of the internet.

In the United States of America, the law governing the use of the internet is called CFAA – Computer Fraud and Abuse Act but it is called ITA - Information Technology Act in India. These laws and their variants in each country govern the use of the internet and computing devices. The cyber law of any country governs Cyber-crime and Cyber-attack.

There has been a misconception about cyber-crime and cyber-attack. Although both are computer related fraud and border on internet fraud, they are different.

Cyber-crime involves the use of a computer to commit crime against individuals e.g. credit card fraud, cyber-terrorism, online dating crime or cyber-bulling. Cyber-attack, on the other hand, is the use of the computer to attack another computer in order to gain unauthorized access into a system or a computer e.g. Man in the Middle (MITM), Virus attack, Malware attack or Denial of service, this can also be called hacking.

Cybersecurity is the process of applying measures to ensure confidentiality, integrity, availability of data, information and services while using the computer. It also means protection of corporate and government networks from attack. It is basically putting up a defence to make a network or an application difficult to exploit.

Cyber-crime protection, on the other hand, tends to focus more on the protection of families and individuals as they navigate the internet. While Cybersecurity can be said to be the general application of measures to ensure online safety for both Cybercrime and Cyber-attack, cyber-crime protection focuses on just the protection against cybercrime.

Below is a cybercrime related scenario and more explanation about Cyber-crime and Cyber-attack.

Case study to differentiate between Cyber-crime and Cyber-attack

On 6th of March 2018, a friend who had applied for various job positions on Indeed, reached out to me that a Human Resources Manager from Reliance Capital sent him a resume approval letter and that he had asked him to make himself available for an interview. The interview would involve responses to some questions through a YouTube link since it was an online job. Meanwhile, the questions are to be sent to him through Google Hangout.

I was a bit sceptical when he told me about the job, but I did not want to discourage him, so I asked him to send me the letter of approval for a quick review. After carrying out a background check on the letter -

which you should always do when a company reaches out to you with an offer of employment - I discovered that the job in question did not match his skill set. The phrasing of the letter was also a giveaway, which convinced me that the bad guys were pretty much the ones at work.

I expressed my misgivings and suspicions about the content of the letter, but he did not indulge nor believe me. After a series of explanations, I told him to play along with the company and do whatever they ask him to do. I equally advised him to be careful not to send any sensitive information or click any link they send to him. I pleaded with him to send me the transcript of the interview when he is done.

The company asked him to put up a YouTube video to respond to some questions sent to him via Google Hangout. He was also instructed to send the YouTube link to the video to ascertain his fitness for the job. Now, keep in mind that all the questions were sent through Google Hangout. That sounds strange, right?

He was also briefed about the company, the benefits, and his job responsibilities, all via Google Hangout chat. Below are the screenshots of the organisation's requests, including the first letter of approval that he got before the interview.

RESUME APPROVAL

kyle@rogersawlaw.com

Mar 5, 2018, 11:40 AM

to

Dear Applicant.

Congratulations! Your resume had been reviewed and you are contacted for an online interview for the jobs opening. Currently we have urgent openings in Reliance Capital.

CURRENT OPENINGS ARE :
1. Data Entry Clerk, Accounting Clerk,Accountant,Payroll,Administrative Assistant,Office Assistant,Bookkeeper,IT Jobs,Customer Service,Project Manager,Marketing Sales and Medical biller .
SKILLS REQUIRED:
≠ Fresher s / 0 - 12year of experience
≡ Any Graduate/B.E/B.Tech/MCA/BCA/PGDCA or Diploma Holder
≡ Immediate Joining
≡ Troubleshooting Desktop Support.
≡ Proficient in Microsoft Office and Excel. Quickbooks knowledge is a plus.
≡ Good Communication and interpersonal skills

To proceed with the interview, You are required to set up a Gmail account (www.gmail.com) then download the app from your app store i.e smart phone and for PC you can download one from the Gmail webpage www.google.com/hangouts to download the app. If you got one already use it, add Mrs Cheryl Nicholson the HR.Manager to proceed, here is the ID (cheryl.nicholson341@gmail.com) for the interview/briefing and comprehensive job details.

Your verification code is M244860-9, this would serve as your identification number throughout the online hiring process. We look forward to having you interviewed.
Date and Time:Asap/9:00-3:00 PM
Job Location: Online/ Work from home
Benefits:
* Compensation: $23.50/hr
* Paid Training provided
* Health insurance, 401k
Best regards
HR Manager.
Reliance Capital Recruitment Team
www.reliancecapital.co.in

First letter of approval before interview

Source: Google email

The first part of the interview questions as typed out by the HR Manager

Source: Google Hangout

Cheryl Nicholson
1) Have you ever worked from home or online before? How many hours do you intend to dedicate to this job position daily?

2)How do you handle stress and pressure?

3)Describe a difficult work situation / project and how you overcame it.

4)Do you have a computer, printer and a fax ?

5)Are you currently employed?

6)What are your goals for the future with the company if employed?

The second part of the interview questions as typed out by the HR Manager

Source: Google Hangout

Cheryl Nicholson
7)What do you think you can do better for us than the other applicants?

8) How would you like to be Paid? Weekly or Bi-Weekly?
 What means of payment do you prefer? Direct deposit, Check, Wire Transfer?

9) What Bank Do You Operate with to see if it tallies with the company's official salary payment account?

10) What's your clerical speed? Do you have an idea of how to use MS excel? What is your highest educational diploma? When did you receive it?

11) Are you willing to work flexible or long hours?

12) What work have you done that involved working with sensitive or confidential issues.?

About the company as typed out by the HR Manager Cheryl Nicholson

Source: Google Hangout

Cheryl Nicholson
The name of our company is Reliance Capital. Reliance Capital, a constituent of Nifty Midcap 50 and MSCI Global Small Cap Index, is a part of the Reliance Group. It is amongst India's leading and most valuable financial services companies in the private sector. Reliance Capital has interests in asset management and mutual funds; life, general and health insurance; commercial & home finance; equities and commodities broking; wealth management services; distribution of financial products; asset reconstruction; proprietary investments and other activities in financial services. We are located at
6th Floor, North Wing, Off Western Express Highway, Santa Cruz East, Mumbai, Maharashtra - 400055, India.
You can visit the company at www.reliancecapital.co.in for more information. You may review the website while we proceed.

Benefits of the job as typed out by the HR Manager Cheryl Nicholson

Source: Google Hangout

Cheryl Nicholson
Benefits for eligible F-T & P-T employees include: Work/Life Balance, Health & Dental, Community Involvement / Matching Gifts Program, Tuition Reimbursement Assistance & Education Life Works, Employee Stock Purchase Plan, Employee Wellness and 401k plans. Paid Time Off and Holidays with Generous Company Discounts.

This is strictly an online and work from home job You will be paid $12/hr during training and $23.50 after your 2 weeks training session. You will receive your payment Biweekly via check or direct deposit depending on your convenience. You will be working 40-45 hours weekly and if you are employed you are going to be working as a full-time employee and not an independent contractor...

Essential job responsibilities as typed out by the HR Manager Cheryl Nicholson

Source: Google Hangout

Cheryl Nicholson
HERE IS THE ESSENTIAL JOB DUTIES AND RESPONSIBILITIES OF AN IT PERSONNEL:
*Ability to analyses and report clearly any technical issue (software and hardware) that any call-center member could face.

*Installation and maintenance of used software, systems, and network.
Improving user's usage of the resource by sharing good practices.

*Maintaining and upgrading the components of the network, desktop and server, networks components.

*Diagnosing the user's issues, fixing them and making a proposal to prevent the same behavior and improve the availability of the resources.

*Provide the Line Manager with as accurate and precise estimates as possible for assigned task duration, along with confidence levels and foreseeable dependencies.

*Attend daily meetings.

*provide the required guidance to the call-center members.

*Ensuring the respect of company policies in IT resources usage

The screenshots above are the transcripts of the conversations they had on Google Hangout during the first part of the interview. I decided to scan the URL that the Human Resources Manager sent him using different vulnerability scanners. It turned out to be a legitimate website, though the hosting was unknown, and only the IP Address was visible. See the image below:

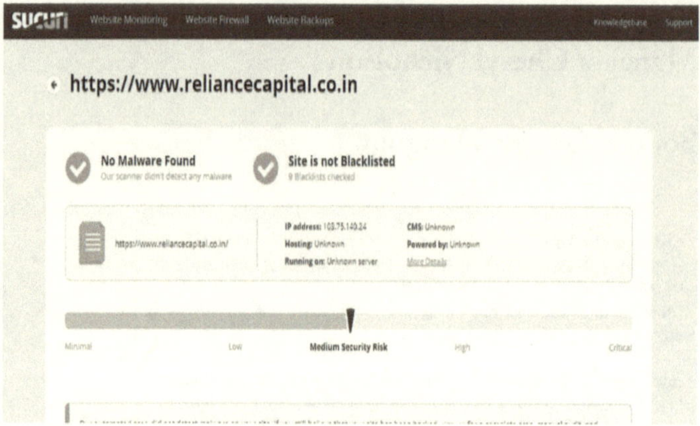

This is a vulnerability scanner used to check if a website is not blacklisted and to see if a website does not have Malware.

Source: https://sitecheck.sucuri.net/results/https/www.reliancecapital.co.in

Further investigation revealed that the lady was a scammer. Then, we thought that it could probably be a guy using the name of a lady Cheryl Nicholson to scam people. She told my friend that the recruiting company she works for has her headquarters in India but that she was communicating from the US. That sounded illogical. After the first part of the interview, we decided to carry out more research about her.

Instead of sending her the link to the YouTube video to get responses to the questions she asked on Google Hangout, we sent her a different YouTube link that has been modified using IP Logger, pretending it was the link to the interview questions just to get her location. See screenshot below:

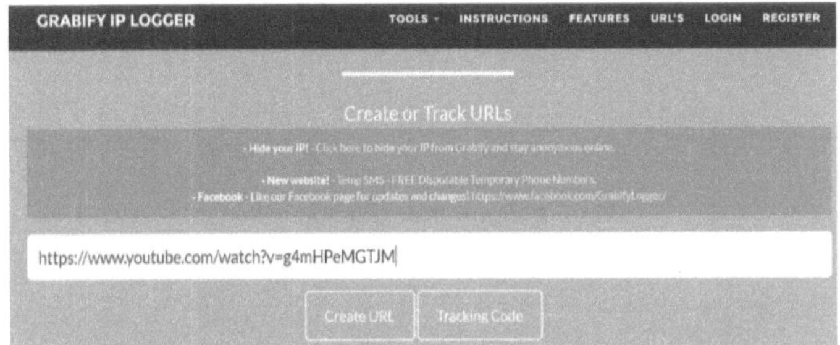

Grabify IP Logger is used to create and Track IP Address

Source: https://grabify.link/

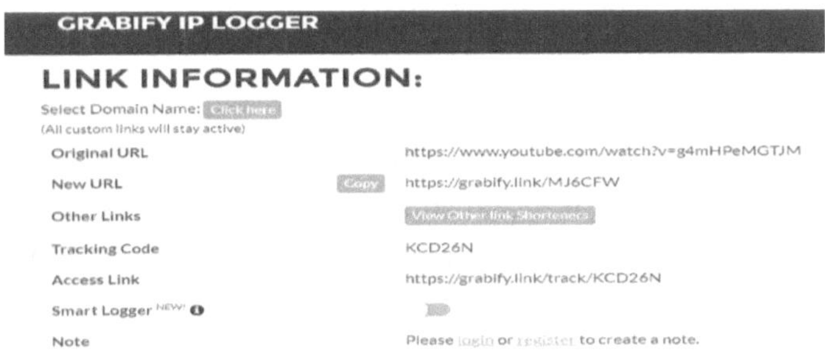

Link Information after being shortened

Source: https://grabify.link/track/F5TRQ1

We used the link to grab her IP Address and then we saw her location from the IP logger. We then used the WHOIS.NET, a query response protocol, to confirm the information of her ISP.

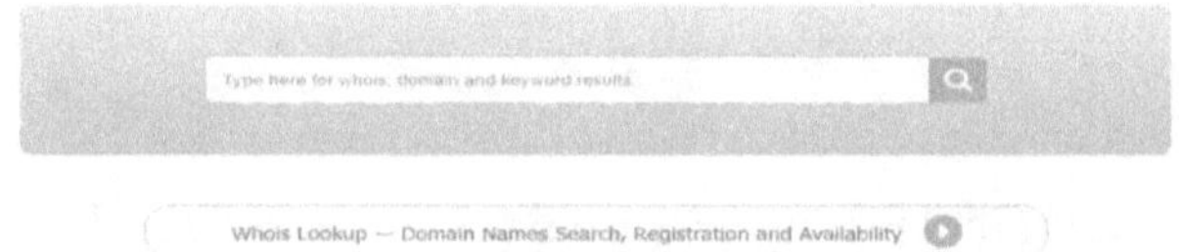

A query response protocol used to query databases that store IP address block worldwide

Source: https://www.whois.net/

From the IP Logger, we discovered that she sent the link to almost five people from different locations and we were able to tell that this person was in Ghana but has some other scammer-friends in South-Africa, Ukraine, Malaysia and Indonesia.

Looking at this crime, it does not involve some of the precautionary measures that you are typically advised to take to avoid online dangers such as installing an anti-virus, operating system updates, two factor authentication, or data encryption, amongst others. It does not involve any of the precautionary measures mentioned in the introductory part of this book either.

The cybersecurity measures mentioned earlier could not help my friend in this case. This shows that not all cyber related fraud has to do with trying to gain unauthorized access but can simply be an attempt to obtain under false pretences using the computer.

It is important to know that most of the cybercrimes that exist are very simple to figure out and do not involve much technicality.

You can easily find out the truth if someone is trying to play a fast one on you, if you put in the effort to do your due diligence about the person on the other end. There are many tools you can use to research a fraudster and you do not need too much technical knowledge to do it.

For instance, you would know that someone is trying to scam you if you received a message from an unknown person that your PayPal account has been compromised when you do not even have a PayPal account.

Tips you need to know about an online scam

1. Too good to be true: If it sounds too good to be true, then be careful because it could be a bait to catch you.
2. Poor grammar: Look at the grammar very well, most times they are poorly constructed.
3. Money: The motive behind everything is money, though they might not make this known initially.
4. Fear inducing: They might try to scare you to act promptly on what they are offering, and sometimes threaten you in subtle ways; do not fall for it.
5. Urgency: Act Now! Urgent! They will often use expressions like this to spur you into action.
6. Personal Information: Do not offer your personal and especially confidential information via online platforms.

CHAPTER SIX

SECURING BANK INFORMATION

Online banking makes life easy. It is faster and convenient to send and receive money while transacting business activities but there is a lot of danger that comes with online banking especially with the use of a credit and debit card to make payments.

When you are connected to the internet, hackers can gain access to your computer and mobile devices via techniques like Man in the Middle, Vishing, Phishing and malwares such as keyloggers and spyware that hide in the background and record keystrokes, passwords, and card details.

There are various ways that cyber-criminals can access your bank account. Cyber-criminals have modified the way they carry out a scam, especially pharming, which involves the practice of redirecting internet users to a website that mimics or replicates the appearance of a legitimate website. Note that email phishing can result into pharming if a user clicks a link and is redirected to a website landing page that has been compromised.

WAYS CYBER-CRIMINALS CAN GAIN ACCESS INTO YOUR BANK ACCOUNT

Internet banking

Both internet banking and Mobile bank banking are similar because they use the internet. While internet banking uses a website, mobile banking uses a mobile application that is available on the app store of the phone.

Bad actors have developed a strategy to either "pharm" a website or spoof a mobile banking application. Pharming works through the link that is sent to the email but Mobile bank spoofing involves the design of a replica bank app, which can be uploaded on a website so that it can be downloaded by an unsuspected user or the customer of a bank.

Another tricky approach to mobile banking fraud is the use of the mobile bank Trojan, a malicious software that scans your phone for a banking app, to steal your information.

How to guide against internet banking scam

1. Never search for the website of your financial institution on Google, visit the URL directly.
2. Always type in the URL of the bank directly into your web browser. Attackers can now optimize a pharmed or a compromised website that when you search for the website URL, it directly brings out the one for the bad actors.
3. Download the Mobile App directly from the App store.
4. Download the mobile app directly from the App store and while you do, always pay attention to the duration of the download. Most times, some of this banking Trojan malware downloads faster than the normal App.
5. Never allow any permission seeking App. This means that if an App keeps asking permission during downloading it could be from the bad actors.

Email Phishing and Vishing

One of the most interesting things about the bad guys is that they think ahead all the time. They have escalated the way they use this method to steal login credentials. They now hack the email account of a legitimate person you know and thereby send you an email through the person's email account so you would believe that the email is coming from your cousin or your friend. Recently, a South Carolina American woman fell victim to this scam to the tune of $60,000.

Vishing is the direct meaning of what email phishing represents but this is usually done on the phone. Instead of sending an email, the bad actor calls you directly pretending to be calling from someone you know or from your financial institution. They mask their intentions in officiality or personality so you could divulge your sensitive account information.

How to guide against Email Phishing and Vishing

1. Always try to confirm whoever sends you a link. That is, confirm from the person reaching out to you not through the email but through other means, like their phone number.

2. Use VirusTotal or Sucuri, a vulnerability scanner, to see if the link has not been compromised by the bad actor.
3. Use true caller app on your phone to know if the person calling is not a scammer.
4. Always apply common sense.

Key loggers

This is a very silent method through which an attacker can gain access into your bank account by using a malware such as keyloggers. Keyloggers are the type of malware that record what you are typing and then sends the information back to the cyber-criminal. You can download malware unknowingly when you want to download an application. It can hide on your device and then start recording keystrokes which the criminal gets to break into your bank account.

How to guide against Malware e.g. Keyloggers

1. Install anti malware such as Kaspersky, Bitdefender, Bullguard, etc.
2. Activate your windows OS firewall Defender.
3. Use 2-factor authentication if your bank allows it. This makes it difficult for criminals to mimic your authentication code.

Man in the Middle Attack (MITM)

Just as the name implies, bad actors use this type of attack to intercept communications between you and the website of your financial institution.

This has to do with taking advantage of a porous or unsecured server and thereby analysing the data packet passing through it using a packet sniffing tool such as Wireshark to analyse the information between an unsecured server and the owner of the bank account. When login details are sent over the network, the cybercriminal sniffs out the details.

This attack is not only limited to this, it can also be done using Domain Name Server (DNS) poisoning which involves poisoning the URL of your financial institution so that when it is visited, you will be routed to a different website that looks exactly like the legitimate website

How to guide against Man in the Middle Attack

1. Do not use a public Wi-Fi to log into your bank account: Avoid using Wi-Fi from the library, coffee shop, airport, etc. to log into your bank account. If you need to do something urgent, use your mobile data

or make sure the traffic is secured using a VPN.

2. Always ensure that there is encryption on every website you are visiting. Check the top of the website where you have the URL to see if it contains the website certificate and the encryption green padlock which can be HTTPS, SSL, TLS.

Spyware

This is also a malware this is hidden under your web browser to gather sensitive information. This gets attached to the internet web browser when you download something online.

To check if your Chrome browser has a spyware, click the three dotted line on your browser. Go to extensions and delete any software that you are not familiar with that is attached to your browser.

How banks and ISPs can help to arrest criminals

It is unfortunate that these days, banks help online fraud to thrive, all in the name of not wanting to breach the privacy protocol signed by a criminal who has moved money from another person's account into his own account.

Here is something interesting to note, the financial institution and ISP can help to give meaningful information on how a cyber-criminal can be arrested using information available to them.

This is a good security tool but is often used by hackers to sniff a data packet on the network.

Source: www.wireshark.org

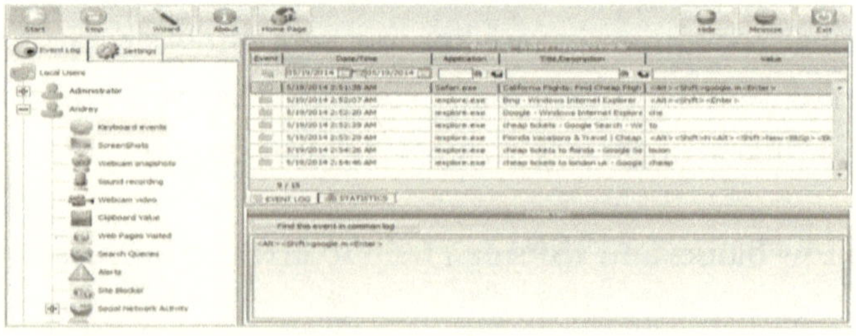

Keylogger is used to save the information of what has been sniffed on the network, especially password information.

Source: https://www.geckoandfly.com/17868/ best-free-keylogger-for-windows-mac-android- ios-to-monitor-your-kids-facebook/

TIPS on keeping your bank account safe

1. Never use a public computer to access your online account.
2. Use strong passwords and change them periodically.
3. Enable 2-factor authentication i.e., use your phone as a token to log in to your account or request a token from your bank.
4. Lock Credit or Debit card when not in use for a long time. This feature is typically available on your mobile bank app.
5. Even on your personal computer, clear cookies, cache and browsing history.
6. Never use a public Wi-fi to log in to your account for any reason, use your mobile data instead.
7. Use a VPN such as Cyber-Ghost, Express-VPN, Norton Wi-Fi Privacy, Private VPN on your PC and Phone.
8. Download Apps directly from the Play-store or Apple store.
9. Sign off appropriately from your account and x-out the page when logging out.
10. Always use your credit card for online an transaction and not your debit card.

11. Ignore requests for too much personal information.
12. Be careful what you sign up for.
13. Never permit cookies from any website.
14. Disable auto-filling of your information from your browser.
15. Stop using checks because it contains all the information that a hacker needs.
16. Sign up for e-statements. Paper statements can get lost and put your account at risk if the sensitive information contained in it gets into the wrong hands.
17. Use a biometric login.
18. Keep your phone and PC locked if you are not using them.
19. When doing necessary security patches on your device, be sure it is coming from the right source.

CHAPTER SEVEN

TYPES OF INTERNET FRAUD

There are more than 50 types of internet fraud. The common ones are:

1. Online dating
2. Credit card Scam
3. Employment Scam
4. Microsoft Technician Scam
5. Amazon Prime Scam
6. Card Skimming Fraud

Online Dating

According to a report by the FBI, millions of people have fallen victims to an online dating scam, especially Americans. People who use dating apps or social networking sites to meet people all over the world, many times, instead of finding romance, people may end up with fraudsters who trick them into sending money to them to solve an urgent problem which might appear very real.

The fraudsters do not engage much computer technicality, but they use lies and intelligence to carry out this evil act. You need to be careful when you meet people online because you can never tell their exact intention.

Below are some of the expressions that these scammers use to swindle their victims

1. Working in the Military as a soldier.
2. Working on the oil rig as an Engineer.
3. Working in an international Organization as a doctor.
4. Payment for mother's medical bill.
5. Payment for plane ticket.
6. Payment for visa or for an official document.

If you meet someone online and after a few weeks or months of dating, the person is trying to use any of the above to get money from you, take note that the person might be a fraudster. Their intents may not be easy to decipher when the relationship is just starting but as time goes on, if you pay attention to details, you will be able to tell especially when their statements do not add up.

You do not need any technical experience here; all you need is to put your brain to work.

Key things to note in an online scam

1. The fraudster always wants to talk through email or text message instead of the dating site message service.
2. The scammer sends a lot of romantic text messages that make him come across as endearing.
3. They sometimes claim to be originally from the US but have been transferred to another location for work.
4. Some of them would never want to talk on video because they always use the picture of a beautiful lady or a handsome guy to perfect the scam.

The Federal Trade Commission Recommendation for online scam

1. Report online dating scams to FTC, your local FBI field office, the FBI's IC3 (https://www.ic3.gov/default.aspx) and your state Attorney.
2. Do not wire money to a stranger regardless of what they say to convince you.
3. Do not try to help anybody you met online to carry out an online transaction, whether to pay for something or send money to a third party.
4. Always be vigilant.

Credit card scam

A credit card scam is becoming more common. This happens when your card information is stolen and compromised. At this point, you may notice a few extra-charges on your account.

A credit card scam is not the same as identity theft where you have all the sensitive information such as Address, Social Security Number, and Birth Date stolen, and the fraudster continues to use it for a long period of time.

Below are some of the strategies you can use to avoid credit card scam

1. Avoid credit repair promise.
2. Do not click any link you are not familiar with in your mailbox until you confirm it is from the credit card company.
3. Do not give your social security number or any sensitive information to anybody on the phone.
4. To avoid downloading malicious software, download from the credit card platform or from an appropriate platform like Play store and the APP store.
5. Always check the statement and receipt closely and report any unfamiliar charges on your card.
6. Monitor all your spending by enabling credit and debit alert on your phone.
7. Be extra careful when giving out card information.

Employment Scam

A lot of people have fallen victim to this scam multiple times because of the methods scammers engage in to perfect their fraudulent plans while taking advantage of people's need to secure jobs.

Scammers go as far as creating website pages and job board accounts like Indeed, Monster, Career Builder and LinkedIn to mention a few. They post jobs on these platforms and when people apply for the jobs, they try to make their process real by conducting interviews using Google Hangout.

They trick people into believing that they are a real company ready to employ them, usually offering a flexible work from home plan with juicy pay packages.

The most used platform by scammers to perpetrate this fraud is Google Hangout. This is because this platform makes it difficult for people to trace them. They contact people through emails, social media messages, Robot calls, letters, and fake cheques to be delivered to an unknown person.

After they have perfected the employment procedure which involves telling you that you have been employed, they will send a cheque to your address for the purchase of your work tools like a printer, telephone, ink, printing papers among others. Before the cheque gets delivered, they will then ask you to send some money to an unknown person whom they will make you believe is also one of their long-term employees. They will likely mention to you the amount on the cheque that has been sent to you, for instance, $8,000. The essence of this is to keep you unsuspecting when they ask you to send $3,000 to another employee as you are likely to think you would get back your money when you eventually receive the cheque. I assure you, the cheque is fake.

Strategies for avoiding employment scam

1. Verify job listings before you apply. This must be done thoroughly as scammers sometimes use real company names. Check the company's website to be sure.
2. Whenever any company contacts you on Indeed or any other job board for a job interview, always read reviews on the internet about that company.
3. Read as many reviews as possible; scammers write good reviews about themselves.
4. Avoid job listings that say, 'no experience required'.
5. Never give out information such as your SSN, bank account details, phone number and email for direct deposit or whatever reason if you do not trust the source.

6. Never take money order as a form of payment.
7. Avoid job listings that require no qualification.
8. Never wire money through Wester Union, MoneyGram, or any other service to a stranger.
9. Know that a real company will not just come out of the blues and offer you a job just like that.
10. Never send Amazon or any other gift card to anyone you do not know.

Microsoft Technicians Scam

You may receive a call directly on your phone from an unknown person claiming to be an engineer or a technician representing a software company like Microsoft. Be aware that the call ID might be spoofed to reflect legitimate support phone numbers and make their lies look very genuine. Do not fall for this.

They might ask you to install an application or enter some commands on your PC that will give them remote access to your device. Some of them monitor your browsing history to determine the difficulties you have with your device, if any.

Apart from this, a scammer might also go as far as making an exact copy of the website of a software company and then add their number to the website after optimizing it such that when you search for the software company, the cloned website will pop up since it is highly optimized. When you call the number, they can then control you to gain remote access to your device.

The latest scam involves a scammer sending an error message to your browser when you visit a website. They put the browser on full screen and display a pop-up message that won't go away which locks your browser then the fake error message tricks you into calling a displayed number on the screen suggesting that you should call the technical assistant.

Below are some of the strategies you can use to avoid Microsoft Technicians Scam

1. Know that Microsoft will never call your number to offer to fix your laptop and thereby request your personal information.

2. Any communication with Microsoft must be initiated by you.

3. Do not call the number on your browser pop-up, the Microsoft warning does not include a phone number.

4. Download software only from the official vendor website or the Microsoft store.

5. Always configure your browser to block a lot of known support scams. Using window defender is also a good option.

6. Uninstall all applications that scammers instructed you to install if you have previously granted them access.

7. Always use your credit card for online payment because you can reverse any unauthorized payment on your credit card.

8. Use www.microsoft.com/reportascam to report the Microsoft scam.

NEW SCAM ALERT!!!

ADWARE AND INTERNET SCAMS

Pop up Message used by Microsoft Technician Scam. Report every Tech Support Scam to the Federal Trade Commission

Source: https://www.consumer.ftc.gov/articles/how-spot-avoid-and-report-tech-support-scams#Scammed

Pop up Message used by Microsoft Technician Scam. Report every Tech Support Scam to the Federal Trade Commission

Source: https://www.consumer.ftc.gov/articles/how-spot-avoid-and-report-tech-support-scams#Scammed

The Amazon Prime Scam

There are many types of Amazon Prime Scam. You might receive a call that your Amazon Prime subscription is due for payment even when you do not have any Amazon subscription. When you tell the caller that you are not subscribed, you will be asked to press any key from your phone if you would like to cancel your subscription after which you will be transferred to another person who will request your account details and card information.

Some other amazon scams include, but are not limited to, the following: Amazon Gift Card Scam, Online listings from fake Amazon Seller Scam, Amazon job offer scam, The Amazon Phishing Scam, The Discount Voucher Scam, to write an Amazon review scam.

Below are some tips to avoid Amazon Scams

1. Do not pay attention to an unknown person telling you that you have a security problem with your Amazon Prime Subscription.
2. Do not call numbers off the internet claiming to be Amazon Prime as all the

numbers have been optimized by scammers who will try to get your card information.

3. If you notice any charge on your bank account, always alert your bank, and get a new debit or credit card or request to close your account and open a new account if the situation requires this.

4. Do not click unknown links in your emails from your inbox and text messages. Delete any link you are not familiar with.

5. Always check if you are on the right Amazon landing page when you are shopping online.

6. Do not shop online with your debit card. Always use your credit card.

7. Never listen to any unknown person that asks you to download Team Viewer or any other app to help you resolve an account issue or a subscription issue.

8. Do not give your card information and account details to anyone, especially when the call was not initiated by you.

Card Skimmer Fraud

Credit or debit card skimming is a type of theft that involves fraudulent charges on your account because of scammers or crooks using a device to steal card information at a legal credit or debit card transaction spot.

When your card is swiped through a skimmer, the device captures all your information on a magnetic stripe, the stripe contains the card number and expiration date with the credit card owner's full name.

You need to be careful because the skimmer of an ATM machine can be removed and replaced by scammers to steal your information. Apart from using a skimmer, a small camera can also be used to capture card information during an ATM transaction.

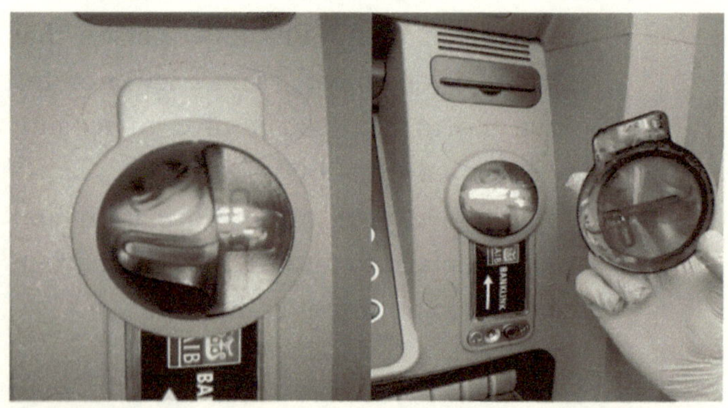

Card skimmer and installed camera to monitor pin.

Source: https://www.engadget.com/2014/07/28/
credit-card-skimming-explainer/

Below are some tips to avoid Card Skimmer Fraud

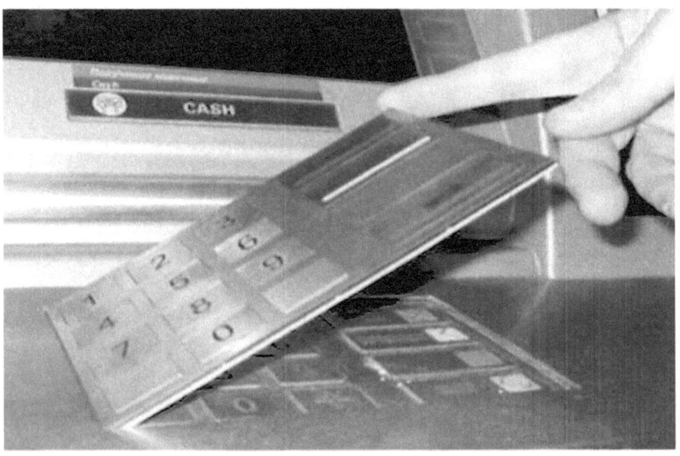

Card skimmer and installed camera to monitor pin.

Source: https://www.engadget.com/2014/07/28/
credit-card-skimming-explainer/

Below are some tips to avoid Card Skimmer Fraud

1. Always check for skimming devices around you when you want to make payments.
2. Do not allow your card to be taken away from the spot where you want to make payment.

3.   Always check ATMs before using them, to ensure there are no protruding parts because of positioned cameras or skimmers.
4.   Do not allow anyone help you clean the magnetic strip on your credit or debit card.
5.   Contact your bank immediately if you think you have fallen victim to skimming.

Cyber-fraudsters now take gift cards as a means of payment from any part of the world because there are many websites such as www.cardcash.com that can help to convert it to any currency so when an unknown person is asking you to send a gift card you should always suspect foul play. Microsoft Technicians scam, Amazon Prime Scam and US benefit scam do this most of the time.

CHAPTER EIGHT

TYPES OF CYBER-ATTACK

There are two types of cyber-attacks. The one with high severity and technicalities that target companies and the one with low severity and technicalities that target individuals.

High severity attacks also target individuals in a way. For instance, when a DDOS (Distributed Denial of Service) attack was launched on Facebook, Equifax, Yahoo, and Capital One, the aim was to steal people's data.

Since this book is concerned with giving precautionary measure and general rules for online safety, privacy, security, and anonymity, we will list out the high technicality attacks and discuss more of the attacks with low technicalities.

Cyber-attack with many technicalities includes:

1. Distributed Denial of Service Attack
2. Drive-by attack
3. Password attack
4. Man-in-the-middle (MitM) attack
5. SQL injection attack
6. Cross-site scripting (XSS) attack
7. Eavesdropping attack
8. Malware attack

Cyber-attack without many technicalities

Social Engineering:

Social Engineering is a cyber-security attack that involves the use of deception to make people share confidential information to be used for malicious purpose or intent.

This type of attack is what cybercriminals use to carry out a data breach. Below are some of the common social engineering attacks:

Phishing:

This is a cyber-attack where the attacker uses manipulated emails as a tool to trick the recipient into believing that the email they received is coming from a genuine source. It could be a disguised email from their company, bank, family, and friends. It requires the user to click a link or download an attachment.

Phishing is dangerous because the attacker pretends to be the real person in order to steal data, it is one of the oldest forms of cyber-attack. The word "Phish" comes from the idea of throwing a bait hook to deceive the intended person.

Phishing techniques

1. Emails are sent with a link redirecting you to a spoofed/hacked website.
2. Login page is changed to direct you to a credential stealing script.
3. A legitimate website or email is cloned to steal passwords and credentials.

Example of how phishing happens using Z-Shadow

Z-shadow is a special website that provides various kinds of links like a real official website but in a "phished" or manipulated form. This is a website that contains the landing pages for login to all well-known social media pages with phishing links.

An attacker copies links from Z-shadow websites and then sends it to a user in order to trick them to get their login credentials.

Z-shadow is used to create a clone of an official account or pages on platforms such as Facebook, Instagram, Twitter and even the web WhatsApp page.

Different Links used to carry out phishing attack.

Sources: www.z-shadow.info

The cloned page always looks very similar to the official page thereby tricking the victim. When you take a careful look at the URL, you may be able to identify that there are differences between the URL for the official website and the phished one. It is called a phishing attack when the email is sent and you and reveals your confidential information but then, two forms of attack are involved by the time the link takes you to a cloned website for your information to be stolen. This is called pharming, phishing and pharming go together most times.

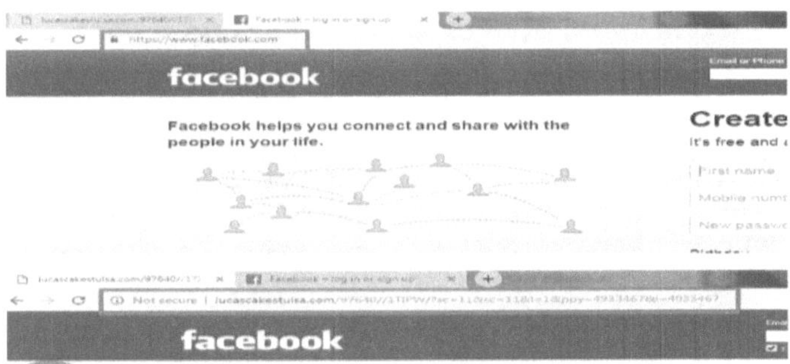

Differences between real and fake Z-shadow URL.

Sources: www.facbook.com and www.z-shadow.info

Once the victim opens the link, they assume that they are on the genuine service provider's page, and they will therefore fill in their credentials to log into their account. Once this happens, the attacker immediately receives all the login credentials as indicated in the diagram below

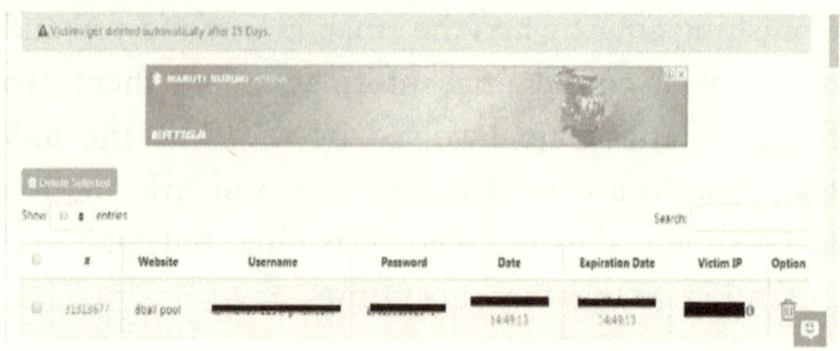

When Z-shadow captures victim's information
Source: www.z-shadow.info

How Hackers use Z-shadow to get victims

1. Create Account from www.z-shadow.info
2. Copy link of the social media page they want to send.
3. Shorten the URL through a URL shortener.
4. Send to victims using a good strategy.
5. Check the Z-shadow website to see victims' credentials.

NB: If you want to practice with Z-shadow, do not use your real information on the website because Z-shadow does not offer SSL. It is good to change your password periodically because when your account is hacked, hackers use your account to do a lot of different things, when you change your password, this kicks the hacker out of your account.

Safety Precautions against Phishing

1. Check URL very well before entering sensitive information.
2. Compare URL in the link sent with the original website.
3. Contact the person sending you the URL to confirm that you are interacting with the right person.
4. It is a good practice to change your password periodically because when your account is hacked, hackers use your account to do a lot of different things, when you change your password, this kicks the hacker out of your account.

Pretexting

Pretexting is a form of social engineering in which an individual pretends to need the information of his target to confirm the identity of the person. For instance, a fraudster can pretend to be calling from your bank to carry out a survey and then ask you to give your account information.

How to guide against Pretexting

1. Do not give out your information unless you are the one that initiated the contact.
2. Ask your financial institution about the policy or procedure involved in sharing your information especially the one for pretexting.
3. Keep documents with sensitive information at a safe place.
4. Add a password to your credit and debit cards. Change your password periodically.
5. Always shred documents that you no longer need thoroughly.
6. Advise your family members not to divulge sensitive information to unknown persons.

Baiting

Baiting is a social engineering attack that works like phishing. The difference is that it targets a company's computer network.

It involves using something very important or convincing to lure people into carrying out an activity that enables the fraudster to steal or break into a company's defence system or trick an individual to get sensitive information.

The goal of baiting is to destroy the defence system of a company security protocol.

The best way to avoid this kind of attack and other social engineering attacks is by educating yourself. The same precautionary procedure used for phishing should be applied to Baiting.

Quid Pro Quo Scams

This is a social engineering attack that promises a benefit in exchange for credentials or vital information.

For instance.

Oh! You have got a problem with your PC? Can I have your credentials to help you fix it? This will be the response of a Quid Pro Quo attacker. They are always looking out for ways to get your credentials and sensitive information. Always watch out for this, the cyber-criminal most times will offer to help you but, he needs your information for an attack.

Safety Precautions against Quid Pro Quo

1. Never give personal information if you did not initiate the dialogue.

2. Get emails and phone number directly from a company's genuine website.
3. Always be sensitive when you are online and offline.
4. Change your password periodically.

Tailgating

This type of social engineering attack mostly happens within an organization. Here, an attacker uses the electronic login of an authorized person to bypass security restrictions. It means walking into an organization using the access of an employee that has legitimate access.

If you work in an organization that requires access cards into the main building, always be sensitive when someone follows you too closely when you swipe your card. If the person successfully gains entrance using your card and something bad happens, during investigation, you might be invited for questioning or even suffer the consequences of what you never did.

The main safety precaution that is required here is to always remain vigilant to avoid tailgating.

CHAPTER NINE

HOW TO SECURE YOUR INTERNET DEVICES

The devices you use when you surf the internet are prone to being compromised by the bad guys if you do not put precautionary measures in place. The following channels need to be adequately secured to avoid identity theft and any form of unauthorized access:

1. Website
2. Wi-Fi
3. Social Network/Social Media
4. Software
5. USB and other hardware
6. Browsers

Website Security

A website is a collection of pages, files, multimedia content and web resources which are commonly identified with a specific domain name and with an extension published on the web server to be accessed by different people around the globe on the internet. Websites are usually accessed using a program called the browser.

There are different types of browsers; this includes Chrome, Mozilla, Explorer, Safari, Opera Mini, DuckDuckGo etc.

The website works by making use of a browser to send a request to the web server which has a lot of information and then the server sends back the information requested which appears on the website. Despite the speed with which the requests are processed, there are a series of processes that take place before the server responds to the browser, it involves a client and server relationship.

Web access protection and security of password

There have been a series of write-ups about the security of individuals and businesses on websites. The most prominent position is for users to look out for the green padlock symbol or the HTTPS to check if a website is encrypted, especially if you want to shop online.

While it is correct to say that any website with such features is encrypted, it does not mean that your information cannot still be stolen. The encryption - whether TLS, SSL or HTTPS - means that when your information is being sent through a website that has these features, it masks your information as it goes back and forth between the client and the server.

You need to be very careful. Hackers also use a secured website to perform a lot of attack using these TLS, SSL, HTTPS on their website. The best thing to do to avoid falling victim is to research and verify if you are visiting a legitimate website. You can also analyse the URL using Virus-Total if you find the website suspicious.

If anyone sends you a link and you are unsure as to whether it contains viruses, Trojan horse or any kind of spyware, you can quickly look it up on Virus Total to see if it is virus free before you download any files. You can also research other useful tools you can use to research things before taking any action.

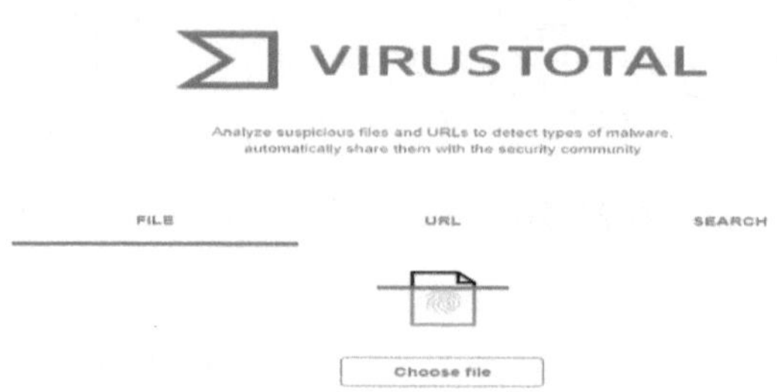

Analyses suspicious files and URLs to detect types of malware and automatically share them with the security community.

Source: https://www.virustotal.com/gui/home/upload

Website Security

1. Make sure all the web apps on the website are up to date.
2. Do not for any reason follow any link that should take you to your bank's platform like following an unknown link 'sent by the bank'. This could be a phishing attack to steal your password and other sensitive

information such as your credit and debit card details.

3. Ensure that you create strong and unique passwords or make use of passphrase to have access to the backend of your website if you have one. You might need to manage your website yourself if someone helped you with the development.

4. Do not follow direct access to upload files to your website.

5. Always use website scanning tools to test your site's security. Use tools like Detective, Qualys, Freescan, Probe.ly, Immunize Security Test, etc.

6. Always research about online safety because in the field of information technology, everything changes all the time.

7. When you discover that a company you are affiliated to has had a breach of security, do not hesitate to change all your login credentials.

8. Always view the certificate of a website after verifying that it is legitimate.

How to check the security certificate of a website

Google Chrome browser

- Click the three dots icon to bring up menu.
- Under the more tools, select Developer Tool.
- Click on the security tab.
- Click view Certificate or click the padlock icon to view certificate.

Internet Explorer

- Click the padlock
- Click view certificate

Firefox browser

- Click the padlock icon
- Click more information
- Click view certificate

Safari

- Click the padlock
- Click view certificate

Wi-Fi Security

Wi-Fi is a technology that uses radio waves to provide network connectivity. It is an electronic facility that allows computers, smartphones, and other devices to connect to the internet or communicate with one another within an area. It uses a wireless adapter to create hotspot.

These are some of the security features you need to be aware of when using a personal and a business Wi-Fi.

1. Use a separate Wi-Fi for your business. On no account should you share your private Wi-Fi with your customers.
2. Always secure your Wi-Fi equipment physically.
3. Always use a Virtual Private Network (VPN) when using public Wi-Fi.
4. Do not connect to public place Wi-Fi, use your mobile data instead. There are rogue access points and rogue Wi-Fi Networks. In general, free WIFI's are not secured.

5. Secure your network using firewalls and hide your Wi-Fi network. There are security features available in most devices which you can use the Setting features in your device.

6. Use Strong encryption such as WIFI Protected Access (WPA1) and Wi-Fi Protected Access (WPA2 or WPA3 when it arrives).

7. Some Wi-Fi access points still use the older WEP (Wired Equivalent Privacy). Avoid using this.

8. Use secured WPA password.

9. Check rogue Wi-Fi Access point.

10. Wireless router these days have 2 Wi-Fi Networks. Use one for your guests.

11. Hide your network name.

12. Enable MAC authentication for your users, that is, you should have an administrator account to control the devices that can connect to your network.

Software Security

Software is a set of instructions that enables a user to interact with the computer. There is system software and application software. System software is the software that is used to operate the computer hardware and application software is the software that is used to perform a task.

The following are some of the security measures to secure software:

1. Ensure that you pay attention to all the message boxes when installing software.
2. Do not install any software using a link from an unknown source. If you want to install an app or software, go to the app store.
3. Companies should have rules and regulations guiding what an employee can install and keep on their computer.
4. Downloading of software can be restricted.
5. Ensure software is up to date and get rid of software you no longer use.

6. Make sure your computer or phone is always set to get automatic updates.

Social Media Security

No doubt, all social media platforms are applications that help people to socialize around the globe. The purpose of any social media platform is to share content and participate in networking while meeting different calibre of people around the world.

There are many things that can go wrong if safety precautions are not put into use when using social platforms. As a matter of fact, if anyone wants to carry out any form of cyber related attack on you, the easiest way to get information about you is to look you up on social media.

Social Media Security and Privacy

Privacy is the safeguarding of your identity online while security is the safeguarding of your data and information to avoid unauthorized access.

The following are some of the security measures to secure social media platforms:

1. If not for business, do not use your real name online. Employers now look you up on social media to have a knowledge of who you are when you apply for a job.
2. Do not use Facebook or Google's Gmail to log in to a website. Use different login credentials.
3. Verify individual identity on social media before accepting their request.
4. Limit who has administrative access to your social media accounts.
5. Set up Two-factor authentication using software such as authenticator.
6. Configure your privacy setting in all your social media accounts to increase security and to restrict the amount of data shared.
7. Always do away with third party applications that are suspicious and always modify your settings to limit the amount of information the application can have access to.
8. Always access your social media account using updated current browsers.

9. Do not for any reason follow any unknown link to your social media platform.
10. Review the privacy settings of an application before use.
11. Be completely invisible by using fake information, especially when you are on social media for fun.

Securing USB and Hard Drive

The USB and the hard drive are parts of the external computing devices that need to be thoroughly scanned for viruses and malware; be careful when dealing with them. The following safety precautions should be put into consideration for securing your computer while using these external devices.

1. Scan all external physical components for viruses and malware before using them on your computer.
2. Disable auto run which enables USB drives to open automatically when you insert them into the computer.

3. Companies should establish strong policies about the use of these hardware components.
4. Do not keep sensitive information in the USB or external drive, save them on the cloud (not disregarding the fact that the cloud has its own disadvantages).
5. Always have a backup for your USB drive

Securing the browsers

Enhancing the security of your browser

The question of the most secured browser has always been on the lips of internet users. It is difficult to really determine which browser is the best. In 2013, a security poll was conducted among browser users, devoted browser users voted unanimously that Firefox is the most secure browser but during the annual Pwn2own hacking contest sometime in March 2014, Firefox security was exploited four times with zero-day attack which then made it one of the least secure browsers at the time.

According to a report by NSS labs, no single browser is bulletproof or secured, if this is the case, then securing the web-browser should be taken seriously. One of the most interesting things about the field of IT is that things evolve daily.

If a solution is provided for the security of an application today, don't be surprised that the bad guys may within the next few days have provided the methodology to compromise it. The field of cybersecurity is a constantly challenging one.

Recommendation and safety precautions

1. Configure security and privacy settings – Block all 3rd party cookies that allow advertisers to track your online activities. For each specific browser, there is always security and privacy setting.
2. Always keep your browsers updated.
3. Sign up for alerts – Set up alerts to stay updated and be current on any emergency security issues. You can create an alert on any browser of your browser choice. Read up and always check YouTube videos to stay informed on this.

4. Be careful when installing plug-ins– Some plug-ins come with malicious software hidden under them to spy on your information, these are called spywares. Check and delete any unwanted features under chrome's extensions because they can put you at risk for some time.

5. Get rid of potentially unwanted programs using an antivirus program such as an alarm, this is one of the best ways to keep PUPs (Potentially Unwanted Program) from hijacking your browser.

6. Install security plug-in to minimize the risk of your browser-insert being compromised.

7. Always clear cookies, browsing history and cache of your browser especially when you are not the owner of the device you are using. This might be a serious security threat to you when you access your online banking app without clearing cookies, cache and browsing history.

8. Be aware that your information is being sold because your browsing history is always tracked by ISPs that inform organizations/companies about what you browse.

9. Always make use of all the security features on your computer and on all your

applications, you can use a VPN such as IP Vanish to secure your data and information.

10. Stay updated on the best browsers that guarantee security and privacy. You can use DuckDuckGo; this browser guarantees privacy and it does not allow your data and information to be tracked.

11. Always check and remove unnecessary extensions on your browser as this could be a spyware to get your account information.

How to remove Spyware from your browser (Google)

1. Click the three dotted lines at the upper right-hand side of your browser.
2. Click 'more tools'.
3. Click 'Extension'.
4. Click 'remove' to take out unfamiliar extensions that could be spyware attached to an app you downloaded.

CHAPTER TEN

DIFFERENCE BETWEEN PRIVACY, SECURITY AND ANONYMITY

In today's digitalized world, there are key terminologies that the internet user should be aware of when engaging the internet and interacting in the global space.

This is important because it gives people an idea of the implication of exposing their data and making their privacy or identity known. Security should be a collective effort; it should not be limited to security professionals. Privacy, security, and anonymity are all issues with online safety.

Security – This involves protection against unauthorized access to data. Security control in devices is put in place to determine and limit who can access the information on the device. Effective security helps to protect data and information to avoid breaches.

As there is improvement in technology and increase in the use of technological devices, security becomes a bigger issue. The wise companies will not take the security of their devices and content casually, especially since there has been a breach in the systems of some well-known companies over the years. For instance, there has been a reduction in the number of people who use Yahoo mail because of the massive data breach that happened to the company in 2016. Also, consider companies like TJ Maxx, Equifax, Capital one, etc.

Security is the major focus of Cybersecurity. If there is no adequate security, the information and the data of a company can be compromised.

Privacy – It is almost impossible to define privacy exclusive of security. This is because privacy has to do with the protection of people's identity and cannot be achieved without securing their information.

While privacy cannot be achieved without security, security can stand without privacy. Institutions like hospitals make security and privacy an important part of health policies.

Hospitals prefer alternative communication systems with their patients using a dedicated medical application to the use of emails and phones to comply with the HIPA (Health Insurance Portability and Accountability) Act to protect PII (Personal Identifiable Information).

In the same vein, security and privacy are also important for merchants dealing with customers' credit and debit card, the Payment Card Industry Data Security Standard (PCI DSS) is responsible for the control of cardholder's data to reduce credit and debit card fraud.

While security measures may be deduced from the system of transmission of data and information, the privacy policy might simply limit a patient's record to a hospital where its accessibility is restricted to only the doctors and the nurses.

Anonymity - Anonymity is the absence of identity. While in privacy, information is kept secret without sharing it with other parties, anonymity involves making the activity public without revealing the identity of the user.

To ensure safety online, it is important to engage the concepts of Security, Privacy and Anonymity.

Below are the six top anonymous browsers that can protect online privacy in 2020:

1. TOR browser
2. First Page
3. Epic Privacy browser
4. Comodo dragon/Ice dragon
5. SRWare Iron
6. Brave

CHAPTER ELEVEN

INCIDENT RESPONSE

Bearing in mind that there is no absolute security, you should be ready to take proactive measures when you notice that your data or account has been compromised. If some of the online safety precautions fail, there are methods that can be applied to cushion the effect of any online scam. Incident Response is a term used to describe how a company or an individual handle a security breach, online identity theft or any form of cyber-attack when they discover it. Consider following the incident response plan below.

Incident Response Plan

1. Have a backup for your PC.
2. Have a dedicated card you use online especially credit card.

3. Do not use the same PIN number for multiple accounts.
4. Do not use the same password for multiple accounts.
5. Have a dedicated Wi-Fi for visitors.

Steps for effective Incident Response

1. **Preparation:** Put a strategy in place on how to act if an attack happens. The incident response plan should come under preparation.
2. **Identification:** Take steps towards tracing and detecting how the breach activity was carried out to plan against a recurrence.
3. **Control:** Engage strategies to stop the damage and prevent further damage from happening e.g. Informing the Federal Trade Commission.
4. **Eradication:** This means restoring the affected device back to their original state while minimizing data loss.
5. **Recovery:** Testing the device to ensure they are fully restored from the attack.
6. **Lesson:** Try to understand the lesson of the scam or attack so you will not fall victim to it again next time.

Response Action

1. Disconnect the affected device from the internet.
2. Restart the device in safe mode.
3. Use an external drive to back-up device if not backed up earlier.
4. Check the computer for possible malware and virus.
5. Change your account credentials.
6. Contact the Credit Bureau if the problem is credit card related (Equifax, Experian, TransUnion).
7. If it is a phishing attack, report to: www.us-cert.gov, www.ic3.gov, or report to Google at 'Report A Phishing' page if Google related

CONCLUSION

The most important thing to note when it comes to the use of electronic devices and online safety is that there are security features available for every hardware and software that is manufactured and there is technical support for each one. Whether it is Wi-Fi, browser, phone, modem, router, computer or camera, the security features that come with a device needs to be studied and enabled before using the device.

Where the security features provided by vendors or a company might not be enough to safeguard your data and equipment, external security features can be deployed. I advise that you explore all available security features in any device before using an external back up security plan.

If you think your device needs an additional security plan, do not hesitate to use it even if it would cost you some money. It is never expensive to keep yourself safe. Many times, ignorance is what makes people fall victim of cybercrime and cyber-attack.

There are basic security features to always have at the back of your mind. These features should always be recurrent:

1. Update Antivirus on all your devices.
2. Backup data from your PC.
3. Use of password manager.
4. Avoid using one password for multiple accounts.
5. Periodic changing of passwords.
6. Use Two Factor Authentication (Not completely reliable).
7. Effect security update and upgrade of devices.
8. Practice safe browsing.
9. Keep privacy and security settings on.
10. Use secure VPN connections.
11. Configuration of Wi-Fi setting.
12. Enable Automatic Operating System patches update.

BOOKS

Vasarhelyi, M. A., & Graham, L. (1997). Cyber smart: Education and the internet. *Management Accounting (USA)*, *79*(2), S32-S32.

Nicol, S. (2012). Cyber-bullying and trolling. *Youth Studies Australia*, *31*(4), 3.

Shraim, I., & Shull, M. (2011). *U.S. Patent No. 7,870,608*. Washington, DC: U.S. Patent and Trademark Office.

Mitnick, K. (2017). *The art of invisibility: The world's most famous hacker teaches you how to be safe in the age of big brother and big data.* Little, Brown.

Manson, D., & Pike, R. (2014). The case for depth in cybersecurity education. *ACM Inroads*, *5*(1), 47-52.

Palfrey, J., Boyd, D., & Sacco, D. (2010). *Enhancing child safety and online technologies: Final report of the Internet Safety Technical Task Force*. Carolina Academic Press.

NOTES FOR FURTHER RESEARCH

https://www.rd.com/advice/relationships/
how-to-avoid-online-dating-scams/

https://www.3debt.org/credit/avoiding-scams/

https://buffered.com/scam-almanac/
employment-scams/

https://docs.microsoft.com/en-us/windows/
security/threat-protection/intelligence/
support-scams

https://www.thebalance.com/
how-credit-card-skimming-works-960773

https://www.tripwire.com/state-of-security/
security-awareness/5-social-engineering-attacks-to-
watch-out-for/

https://www.tripwire.com/state-of-security/
security-awareness/5-social-engineering-attacks-to-
watch-out-for/

http://www.aabri.com/manuscripts/131446.pdf

https://www.social-engineer.org/framework/influencing-others/pretexting/

https://www.linkedin.com/pulse/social-engineering-quid-pro-quo-attacks-mohammad-salman-nadeem

https://blog.mailfence.com/what-is-tailgating/

http://resources.infosecinstitute.com/phishing-dangerous-cyber-threat/

https://resources.infosecinstitute.com/10-most-common-phishing-attacks/

https://www.hiv.gov/blog/difference-between-security-and-privacy-and-why-it-matters-your-program

https://www.android-data-recovery.org/z-shadow-hack.html

https://www.nckprocomputers.com/scam-alerts/

https://digitalguardian.com/blog/what-incident-response

9 789865 626 6 8 3 3